SINCE 1887

MERCY HOME
FOR BOYS & GIRLS

In gratitude for your
faithful friendship to
the boys and girls
of Mercy Home.

Fr. Scott

SEEDS OF FAITH

Faith

SEEDS OF FAITH

Faith

Words of Faith from
NORMAN VINCENT PEALE

Ideals Publications · Nashville, Tennessee

ISBN 0-8249-4635-9

Published by Ideals Publications, a division of Guideposts
535 Metroplex Drive, Suite 250, Nashville, Tennessee 37211
www.idealsbooks.com

Editor, Peggy Schaefer
Designer, Marisa Calvin
Cover photograph: D. Hurst/Alamy Images

Printed and bound in Mexico by RR Donnelley
10 9 8 7 6 5 4 3 2 1

ACKNOWLEDGMENTS
The material by Norman Vincent Peale contained in this book is used
by permission of Guideposts, Carmel, New York.

All Scripture quotations, unless otherwise noted, are taken
from The King James Version of the Bible.

Scripture quotations marked (NKJV) are taken from the New
King James Version. Copyright © 1982 by Thomas Nelson, Inc. Used
by permission. All rights reserved.

Faith is the most powerful of all
forces operating in humanity,
and when you have it in depth,
nothing can get you down. Nothing.

—NORMAN VINCENT PEALE

FOREWORD

Throughout his long career, my father, Norman Vincent Peale, valued no message more than that of the importance of faith in each of our lives. In fact, before the title was finalized, *The Power of Positive Thinking* was called *The Power of Faith*. It was that important to him.

Growing up in the Midwest at the beginning of the twentieth century, Dad learned about faith at his parents' knees and in the pews of small-town churches. Faith in God, country, and fellow man, and the saving message of Jesus Christ filled his youthful days. He learned oratorical skills by listening to the great preachers of the day,

who went from town to town, bringing countless people to faith. He became filled with faith messages, and they never left him.

When the personal call came for him to enter the ministry, Dad was well equipped with deep faith, a gift for communicating, and a love of people. His writings were full of anecdotes of the faith journeys of countless people he met along the way. By their examples, he was able to lead others to a life of faith. His was a great calling, and I think we can all agree that he succeeded.

As you read, I hope you enjoy the messages in this book and that it brings deeper faith into your life.

—*Elizabeth Peale Allen*

If ye have faith as a grain of mustard seed... nothing shall be impossible unto you. —MATTHEW 17:20

$\mathscr{J}$ am constantly amazed at the astonishing power that can be released in people by the simple habit of positive thinking, which is another term for faith.

"But," you may say, "I've tried positive thinking and things didn't turn out right."

What do you mean by "right"? Do you mean as

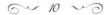

you wanted? How do you know that your idea, the thing you wanted, is in harmony with God's idea? It is my humble belief that when you and I are willing to put ourselves in harmony with God's ideas, without trying stubbornly to force our own way, then things turn out right. Although this does not necessarily mean as we thought we wanted.

"But," you may then say, "there are positive thinkers who suffer pain."

That's right, there are. Sometimes, by the grace of God through positive thinking, pain is eliminated. There are other cases where, by the inscrutable will of God, pain is not eliminated. But the individual rises above the pain until he masters it, and positive thinking has worked again. It does not work by pretending that the pain is not there. Positive thinking is realistic thinking. It always sees the negative, but it doesn't dwell on the negative and nurture it, letting it dominate the mind. It keeps the negative in proper size and grows the positive big.

You may say, "I have known many sick people who tried to heal themselves with positive thinking, and they have died."

That's right! Death is a part of the human experience. Everyone will die. The questions to ask are these: How did they live? How did they die? Full of fear and resistance and terror? Or courageously and gallantly, going into eternity with that glory with which they came from God?

The Gospel speaks to us of the great power of faith. In the Book of Matthew, Jesus tells us that, by faith, we may cause a mountain to be moved. What a word, *mountain*! It means a tremendous obstacle. Everyone has his mountain. "If ye have faith as a grain of mustard seed, ye shall say unto this mountain, Remove hence to yonder place; and it shall remove" (Matthew 17:20).

"If you have faith," says the most reliable document ever written, "nothing shall be impossible."

And how do you release this power? You release it by changing the cast of your thoughts. By practicing belief rather than disbelief.

You probably go along every day affirming, "I cannot do that, I cannot do this." How many times a day do you say, "I cannot do it"? As you repeat that negative thought to your subconscious mind, it will become a fact, because your subconscious mind wants to believe it anyway. Then you come up with a proposition and you hopefully ask your subconscious mind, "Can I, or can't I?" Your subconscious mind will answer that you cannot do it. You have trained it to answer negatively.

Faith sees the invisible,
believes the incredible,
and receives the impossible.

ANONYMOUS

If, over a long period of time, you create in your mind the picture that you cannot, you will inevitably have a picture of yourself failing and, therefore, you will fail. As you think, so are you. You have thought yourself into a state of disbelief in yourself.

You have two powers within you, creative imagination and will. You may summon your will, which will say, "I can." But your creative imagination says, "No, you cannot." In this conflict of opinion, you cannot, because your creative imagination is stronger than your will. This is true because imagination is in the realm of belief, and what you believe in your heart determines what you can or cannot do. If, over a long period of time, you believe that with the help of God you can overcome and you can achieve, then you will get a deep, fundamental, unshakable, unblurrable picture that you can. Your will and your imagination will flow together, and against that power nothing negative can stand.

One of the greatest American authorities on the human mind was the philosopher William James, who said, "Believe, and your belief will in time create the fact." The essayist and poet Ralph Waldo Emerson said, "Beware of what you want, because there is a strong likelihood that you will get it." Get into your mind positive convictions about what you want to be, what you want to become, and what you want to do.

A friend of mine once lost his job. He had a wife and two children. I thought I would comfort him, so I took him out to lunch and said, "I will be glad to help you in any way I can."

"I do not need your help," he replied. "I can handle this problem."

"Who is helping you?" I asked.

"God is helping me," he replied. "There is a job for me. I can see it in my mind's eye." He gave me the exact specifications of the job he wanted.

"You have a wife and two children—how much money do you have in the bank? Have you saved any money?"

"Not much."

"Are you interviewing potential employers?"

"Yes. I see about five people a day, and I get turned down five times a day."

"Doesn't that bother you?"

"No. I realize that I have to be turned down so many times to get this job. I do not know how many times I have to be turned down. But I know if I am turned down five times a day, that is five fewer times I have to be turned down to get the job. And I

In God have I put my trust:
I will not be afraid what
man can do unto me.
PSALM 56:11

will be turned down four or five times tomorrow, four or five times the next day. It may continue a month, two months, three months, but the process just eliminates them. The 'no's' are all behind me and I will get nearer to the person who will say to me, 'Yes, here's your job.'"

One day, my unemployed friend walked into an office and described to the person there the job he wanted. The man said, "The job is here waiting for you. Where have you been?"

Later I saw this friend at a convention where I was to speak. He was the presiding officer during part of the meeting. I asked him, "Where did you get such ideas as that, anyway?"

And this is what he said: "I got it from the Bible. It tells us if you have faith, believe in yourself and in God, and know where you want to go, and then picture it and put it in God's hands, asking if it is His will, you will get God's help and you cannot fail."

If there is still in your mind the idea that you cannot do something, the reason you do not accomplish it is because you are thinking negatively. Start believing, start having faith. And presently you will attain results. It is not by identifying yourself with failure, but by identifying yourself with success, that success and not failure comes to you.

When I stand before a congregation and study the faces of the people before me, I often wonder whether anyone present suffers from a lack of self-confidence. It is the mark of a sophisticated, intelligent person to dissemble, that is, not to reveal in appearance the inner frustrations of his life. So I know that even though it does not appear so on the surface, there may be many who are plagued by self-doubt and feelings of inferiority. This general condition exists throughout the world today.

A university put out a questionnaire among six

hundred students taking courses in psychology and asked them, among other things, to state what they thought was their most pressing, painful personal problem. Seventy percent of them indicated that their worst problem was lack of courage or lack of self-confidence.

What, then, is the secret of self-confidence and courage? It hinges on the kind of thoughts you think. If you nurture negative thoughts over a long period of time, you are going to get negative results. Your subconscious is very accommodating. It will send up to you exactly what you send down to it. If you keep on sending it fear thoughts and self-inadequacy thoughts, that is what it will feed back to you.

It may be that as a child you had experiences which made you doubt yourself, made you shy, withdrawn, reticent, bashful. If you developed such a state of mind as a child, you will have it as long as you live unless you do what it takes to change all that. What you need to do, of course, is to take charge of your mind and begin to fill it with the healthiest, most powerful, most vital thoughts ever formulated. And where do you find these? In the Bible—that's where you find them. The Bible is full of healing thoughts which, if put into your mind, will change your whole condition and fill you with courage and self-confidence.

When you come right down to it, the secret of courage and self-confidence is to fill your life with God. You were created by God and He made you right. If you haven't walked with God, you are making yourself wrong.

One evening, I made a speech to a big gathering of salesmen, and when the meeting was over, I remained on the stage quite a while shaking hands with a lot of people. Over to my left I noticed one man who just stood there waiting. Only when everyone else had gone did he approach me. And

*Your faith is what you believe,
not what you know.*

JOHN LANCASTER SPALDING

he asked, with great intensity: "Can I talk with you a minute?"

We walked backstage and sat down on a pile of lumber. "What's the trouble?" I asked.

"I don't belong to this convention," he explained, "but I heard you were going to talk on how to think positively, and I crashed the meeting. I'm embarrassed to be taking your time, but frankly I'm desperate. I am here in this city for the biggest deal of my life, coming up tomorrow morning. If I fail, that is the end for me. If I don't put this deal together, I am through."

"Now look, my friend," I said, "don't be so

dramatic. Let's hope you do carry off this business deal, but if you don't, tomorrow is another day."

"Oh, but this is my one big opportunity," he insisted. "You mustn't take it so lightly."

"You are too tense, too rigid. In such a state you can't be in full possession of your faculties. Relax. The world is not going to end if you don't put this deal over. Don't get so worked up."

"Well," he said, "I sure would like to know why I always feel so inadequate. I've been this way all my life. Now if my brother had this job to do tomorrow, he would put it over."

"Why are you bringing your brother into it? What's he got to do with it?" I asked.

"He was always the smart one in the family," the man answered. "He's a year younger than I am. When we were in school he always got straight A's. I never got better than a C in any course I ever took."

"What's your brother doing now?" He named the job his brother was doing—a routine job. "It looks to me as though you are doing bigger things than your brother. Maybe he did get A's at school, but I can tell you this: I knew men at college who got straight A's and no one has heard of any of them since. On the other hand, some who only got C's are now leaders in their communities."

"But what am I going to do? How can I get more confidence?"

"As I see it, there are two things you should do. You need counseling to help you learn why you have this deep inferiority feeling. But," I said, "you also need some first-aid things to pull you through this present emergency. I'll give you a couple of those right now. Let's stand up. I can't give you these in a slumped condition.

"Now," I said, "repeat after me these words: 'I can do all things through Christ who gives me the

All I have seen teaches me
to trust the Creator for all
I have not seen.

RALPH WALDO EMERSON

strength.' And I will give you another one: 'If God be for us, who can be against us?' Have you ever heard that before? It's from the Bible."

"No, I never did."

"Don't you read the Bible?"

"No."

"Well, do those words make sense to you?"

"Yes, they do."

"All right, now change the 'us' to 'me' and repeat after me, 'If God be for me, who can be against me?'"

I got him to repeat it several times. I wrote it out on a card for him. I told him, "Now keep thinking this great thought. Think it as you leave this place and walk down the street. Think it when you get up tomorrow morning. Then go to your appointment in a relaxed manner and tell that man honestly why you think what you have to sell is something he needs."

I remember how he pulled himself up straight and looked at me. All he said was, "Okay, doctor."

As he walked away into the night, I stood looking. As he passed under a streetlight, I could see him still holding himself very straight, and I felt sure he was in good shape for the next day. And the outcome proved that he was.

Later we were able to arrange for some counseling for him. And over a period of time he completely changed the color and complexion of his thinking by putting into his mind great words out of the greatest of all thought books.

When you are honest and real and whole, then you have normal courage and normal self-confidence. This is the secret of courage and self-confidence: let God help you to be yourself.

*T*here is a text in the New Testament that is probably one of the greatest gems of truth you will find in the greatest book of wisdom in the world. It is Mark 9:23: "If thou canst believe, all things are possible to him that believeth." Notice that you are offered something tremendous, but there's an "if." "If thou canst believe," then all things are possible. Believing—to the depth at which we are now directing our thought—is hard. It requires mental discipline. It requires self-surrender. It requires giving your whole self to it. It isn't something off the top, or the surface, of your mind. It certainly isn't the glib recital of a creed. But, if you can overcome your doubts and your negativity and really, deeply believe, you can enter into a life transformed, for "all things are possible to him that believeth." This is the magic of believing.

Belief is factual; it is truth. The term "magic" is synonymous with utter wonder. The magic of believing is a manifestation of one of the greatest powers in the universe, the power of thought. By our thoughts, we either create or destroy.

You can build up your life by thinking constructively. You can tear down your life by destructive thinking. What you are this day is the result of what you have been thinking for many years. We do not bear in mind nearly enough the creative and the destructive power of thought.

Suppose, for example, you are a negative thinker. You are full of negative thoughts from morning until night, and you voice them. What are you doing? Something dangerous: you are activating negatives in the world around you. There is a law that like attracts like. I didn't invent that law, but it is there. If you send out negative thoughts, you activate negative influences in the world through the operation of this law of attraction, and you draw back to yourself negative results. There is no other way it could be. On the other hand, if you send out positive thoughts—bright, resplendent thoughts of faith—you activate positive

Jesus said unto him, If thou canst believe, all things are possible to him that believeth.

MARK 9:23

influences in the world around you, and you draw back to yourself positive results.

Let's suppose you think fear thoughts. These thoughts activate fearsome, anxious tendencies in the life around you, and you draw back anxiety results to yourself. But if, on the other hand, you remind yourself, "I am a child of God, and God is with me, so I need not be afraid," you will be sending out positive thoughts of courage and faith, and if you keep it up, you will draw back to yourself thoughts of courage and of faith. We get what we think. The magic of believing brings back to us the great things that a good God gives.

I was in Charlottesville, Virginia, some time ago. In front of the hotel in Charlottesville is a marvelous statue of the famous Confederate General Stonewall Jackson. Once, when Stonewall Jackson was planning an audacious Civil War campaign in the Shenandoah Valley, a timorous general—one of his subordinate commanders—came to him the night before a scheduled forward push. He said, "General, I'm afraid. I'm afraid that this is an improper deployment of our troops. I'm afraid our strategy is not sound. I fear we're going to lose a lot of men."

The great Jackson put his hand on the shoulder

of this commander and said, "General, never take counsel of your fears."

If you take counsel of your fears, your fears will reproduce themselves. If you harbor doubts about yourself and your ability, and think of yourself as inferior, you will get back failures and limitations. It is very serious how we so often defeat ourselves by our thoughts, when, by the magic of believing, we could be winning victories.

One time, after a speech at a convention, a man came up to me and said, rather wistfully, I thought: "I only wish I could believe all that you said about the power of believing."

"Well," I told him, "one way is to practice believing it. And I would suggest you study the passages on faith in the Bible. It's the Bible that tells us: 'All things are possible to him that believeth.'"

"Where is that?" he asked, and I told him he would find it in Mark 9:23. Then he protested, "But you just don't know my problems. I've got a lot of trouble. Being a preacher, you wouldn't understand that."

"Say that again, my friend."

"I've got a lot of trouble," he repeated.

I assured him that I shared his feelings about trouble, but said that when I feel I am having a

Before me, even as behind, God is, and all is well.

JOHN GREENLEAF WHITTIER

hard time, I often think of a line from an old spiritual: "Nobody knows the trouble I've seen. Glory hallelujah!" Yes, we have trouble, but we also have God. So, glory hallelujah! With faith in God we can overcome the trouble.

I finally convinced him to give the magic of believing a try. Like many other executives, he had boxes on his desk for the mail, reports, and papers. There was a box for incoming items, one for the outgoing mail, and a third labeled "Undecided." The "Undecided" box usually had more in it than the other two boxes put together. Now he got a fourth box and put it alongside the other three. And he put on it a label saying, "With God All Things Are Possible." When he found himself faced with a tough problem, he'd write a memo on it and throw the memo and any related papers into this fourth box. There he would leave the matter, believing that, when the problem had to have an answer, God would supply it. He would pray about the situation and surround it with the magic of believing. Some weeks later, he wrote, "It's wonderful, the results I get from this. You can be healed right now, and your healing can start at any time regardless of how serious your condition may appear to you, if you will let go your fears and give God His rightful place in your life."

How can you afford to refuse Jesus Christ when you see every day in your life what faith in Him can produce? This Christ became a reality to me many years ago; and the freedom from pain, from sickness, and from fear, which I have had in the intervening years, is what I am trying to offer you through these words today. What He has done for me, what He has given me, He is willing to give you, if you will try to practice the magic of faith, the magic of believing.

The magic of believing stimulates a wonderful flow of power. Christianity is a fount of power—of the greatest power in the universe. The Bible contains techniques and formulas of power. Jesus, after His resurrection, said to the disciples, "You shall receive power when the Holy Spirit has come upon you" (Acts 1:8, NKJV). That was the beginning of the Christian faith, a promise of power.

How much power have you? Are you living in a great flow of power, or are you living in a miserable little trickle? No matter what your problem, or your difficulty, or your defeat, there is enough power in the magic of believing to overcome any or all of it "if thou canst believe." And you can believe if you will surrender your life to Him.